DISCOVERY GiRLS ❦

THE FARMINGTON COMMUNITY LIBRARY
FARMINGTON HILLS BRANCH
32737 WEST TWELVE MILE ROAD
FARMINGTON HILLS, MI 48334-3302
(248) 553-0300

Fab Girls™ Guide to

Getting Your Questions Answered

Edited by Ellen Pill Blooming, Ph.D.

30036010551123

☞ W9-CNA-865

Discovery Girls, Inc.

CALIFORNIA

OCT 14 2010

Discovery Girls, Inc.
4300 Stevens Creek Blvd., Suite 190
San Jose, California 95129

Fab Girls™ Guide to Getting Your Questions Answered

Copyright © 2007 Discovery Girls, Inc.
All rights reserved. No part of this book may be used, reproduced, or transmitted in any form or by any means, electronic or mechanical, including photocopying, recording, or by any information storage or retrieval system, without permission in writing from the publisher.

The advice in this book is not intended to replace that of girls' parents, physicians, psychologists, teachers, or other experts. It should be used as an additional resource only. Questions and concerns about mental or physical health should be discussed with a doctor or qualified healthcare professional.

Ask Ali illustrations by Aruna Rangarajan.
Book design by Katherine Inouye Lau and Bill Tsukuda.

ISBN 978-1-934766-02-6

Visit Discovery Girls' web site at www.discoverygirls.com.

Printed in the United States of America.

Dedication

Dedicated to the thousands of girls who have taken the time to write to *Discovery Girls* magazine to share your ideas, thoughts, personal stories, and yes, even your problems. All of us who work at Discovery Girls, Inc. have been deeply touched by your letters. You are a constant source of insight and inspiration, and the reason we have created this book.

Acknowledgments

I'd like to send a special thank you to all the girls who have read *Discovery Girls* magazine over the years and have generously shared your thoughts, ideas, and experiences with us. Without you, there would be no *Discovery Girls* magazine and definitely no Discovery Girls books. I feel so very fortunate to have had the opportunity to work with my dedicated and talented staff: Julia Clause, Ashley DeGree, Naomi Kirsten, Katherine Inouye Lau, Alex Saymo, Bill Tsukuda, Sarah Verney, and interns Lyn Mehe'ula, Laura Riparbelli, and Nick Tran. Your enthusiasm and ability to keep your sense of humor while meeting insane deadlines, your willingness to work long hours, your amazing creative energy, and your insistence on always striving to get better and better have meant more to me than you will ever know—my deepest appreciation! Also, a very special thank you to artists Kathleen Uno, Bill Tsukuda, and Rhiannon Cunag for helping bring the Fab Girls to life.

Catherine Lee
PUBLISHER
DISCOVERY GIRLS

Meet the Fab Girls

Carmen

Dallas

Hi! We're Carmen and Dallas Fabrulézziano, but you can call us the Fab Girls! Why "*Fab*"? Well, we came up with that because Fabrulézziano isn't exactly the easiest name to say, and besides, we're totally *fabulous*! Ha, ha—just kidding.

We may be twins, but we're *totally* different. Carmen plans everything down to the smallest detail—from her glamorous outfits to her perfectly edited homework. She **can't live without her personal organizer**—it even helps her remember the birthdays of practically everyone in the eighth grade! Dallas, on the other hand, is too busy coming up with amazing ideas to organize anything. She's **super smart and super creative,** and you can always count on her to tell you the truth—no matter what! But even though we are so different, **we still make a great team.**

No one ever has a tough time telling us apart, and that's what's so absolutely awesome about being a Fab Girl! Even though **we're complete opposites,** we still share that special sisterly bond that makes us **the best of friends**...well, *most* of the time!

So, what exactly are we doing here? Discovery Girls asked us to help you through these **crazy, confusing middle-school years.** And who better to go through them with than a couple of fun Fab Girls who know exactly how you feel? We'll give it to you straight and tell you **everything you need to know.** Like...did you know that Ali (*DG's* advice columnist), receives *thousands* of letters from girls like us? When we heard that, we just *had* to know **what girls wrote about most often.** We'll share what we found out, **so look for us throughout this book!** And remember: With the Fab Girls around, **you're never alone.**

xoxo ♡ carmen & Dallas

Name: Carmen

Hobbies: Acting, reading romance novels, and perfecting my chocolate-chip cookie recipe.

My biggest dream: To win an Academy Award.

I never leave home without: My planner! It's a minute-by-minute outline of my busy days—dance lessons, friends' birthdays, homework, auditions…I'd be lost without it!

Everyone knows: I'll be totally famous one day! I mean, I already had a small part in a movie…

No one knows: I'm actually very shy. When I have to give a presentation in class, I get totally nauseous.

Biggest pet peeve: People who don't RSVP. I'd love to give half my school a crash course in etiquette!

My take on Dallas: She always knows when I'm feeling down, even if I haven't said a word. She helps me think about things in completely different ways, and I'm my old self in no time!

Name: Dallas

Hobbies: Running track, photography, and playing the drums in my band. (I'm the only girl!)

My biggest dream: Yearbook editor today, world-traveling Pulitzer Prize-winning photojournalist tomorrow!

I never leave home without: Painting a tiny star under my right eye...it's my trademark!

Everyone knows: I'm a math wiz. As math team captain, I totally convinced the principal that we deserve jackets this year.

No one knows: I have a crush on the lead guitarist in my band. (But—SHHH! Don't tell!)

Biggest pet peeve: Girls who gossip and judge others. Don't get me started!

My take on Carmen: She's the most thoughtful sister! Every year on our birthday she creates a new scrapbook for me with highlights of my entire year... with doodles and pictures to match.

Contents

When Did Life Get Oh-So-Dramatic?

You're the only girl in your class who has started to develop...so how do you deal with the stares and snickering when it's time to change for gym? You used to have six close friends, but they all dumped you for the popular crowd...and **now you have no one.** You're fine with being "just friends" with guys...so what do you do when your **boy-crazy friends pressure you** to have a *boyfriend*? And then there's the tougher stuff, like **coping with the death of a parent**, being asked to choose between your mom and dad in a divorce, and worrying about a best bud who may be getting hurt by a parent at home...

Whether you're at school, at home, or just hanging with your buds, **drama seems to find you *everywhere*.** No wonder you feel lost sometimes!

It's time to take back your life, girls! Discovery Girls' *Fab Girls Guide to Getting Your Questions Answered* is your must-have book for dealing with life's most pressing problems. At *Discovery Girls* magazine,

we receive thousands of letters for Ali, our advice columnist—many more than we can possibly answer in the magazine. So, here, for the first time, Ali answers more of your questions than ever and tackles your toughest issues.

So press "pause" on the drama that is your life, settle in, and find out how to **deal with your problems** of yesterday, today, and tomorrow—starting now!

The Editors of *Discovery Girls*

Chapter One

Friends

Your BFF dramas most
often revolve around:

- One friend wants to be more popular.
- Jealousy over having other friends.
- Silly fights that get out of control.

Dear Ali,

Ever since I got a part in the school play and my friend didn't, she has been acting very weird. I have been leaving class to practice, and when I get back to class she gives me this mean glare. At lunch, I sit down next to her and I try to talk to her, but she quickly changes the subject and then walks off. My friends tell me that she is talking badly about me behind my back. I don't want to lose a good friend. What do I do?

—Losing My Friend

Dear Losing My Friend,

Unfortunately, it sounds like your friend has a bad case of jealousy. She wanted to be in the play, too, and you made it without her. You've done nothing wrong, but she's having a hard time dealing with her feelings. So what can you do? Try to be sensitive about how difficult this is for her. How would you feel if she'd gotten in and you hadn't? Let her know that you're sorry she didn't get a part, and that you don't want this to affect your friendship. You might even say something like, "Next time you'll probably get a part and I won't!" You could also find out if there are opportunities for her to help with the play. There are important backstage jobs, and they're sometimes even more fun than acting! If you can talk it through, you may be able to help her deal with her jealousy.

ali

Dear Ali,

My friend Kyla is a great friend, but not a lot of people think so. By "a lot," I mean the rest of my friends! I know that Kyla is trying too hard to be popular. She tries to be funny, but she's not. But when you get to know her like I have, you like her the way she is. How can I get her to just relax and show her true self?

-Friend 911

Dear Friend 911,

You are a true friend for taking the time to get to know Kyla and for sticking by her. Keep in mind that you can't make her act differently, but you can let her know what you think. Tell her that she is a terrific person and a good friend, but when she tries too hard to be someone she's not, people can't see how wonderful she really is. Suggest that she stop trying so hard to be liked and see what happens. The rest is up to her!

Unpredictable Friend

Dear Ali,

I have this friend who is so fun to be around when she's happy. But when she's not doing so great, she's the worst person in the world. Half of the time we're best buds, and the other half we're sworn enemies. It's really hard to stay away from her when she's happy. It's like she's so full of life, which draws people to her. But then again, there are those times when she turns on you and becomes the meanest, most selfish girl in school. Another thing is that when I _am_ her friend, I want to tell her everything, even my deepest, darkest secrets. But when she's my enemy, she blabs everything I've told her. What do I do?

—Two-Faced Friends

Dear Two-Faced Friends,

You really have an unpredictable situation here! You can't change your friend's behavior, but you _do_ have control over your own choices. It's time to realize that she's not the kind of friend who will always be there for you. It's okay to enjoy being with her when she's being nice, but you'll have to steer clear of her when she's not. You need to take responsibility for your own behavior—don't mimic her by becoming mean just because she does. Stay your friendly, nice, and trustworthy self, no matter what. Avoid her when she's in one of her bad moods, and resolve to not tell her any of your secrets, since you never know when or what she will blab. If you can live with these rules, you'll be okay. If not, you might just need to move away from this oh-so-dramatic friendship entirely.

ali

We're best buds—and sworn enemies!

Dear Ali,

I don't have friends! It isn't fair. When there is a project at school, nobody wants to be with me. I used to have six friends, but they all dumped me to become popular. I want a friend who I can talk to when I'm upset or else I'll go nuts! I think I should have a party so girls could notice that I'm a great friend. Please! Please! Give me advice on finding friends!

—Friendless

Dear Friendless,

Friendships can be so confusing, and sometimes it's hard to pinpoint what went wrong. You might want to take one of the girls aside and ask her why you're not being included anymore. The key is to tell her—nicely—that you really want to know. Then, do your best to listen to her answer without getting defensive or telling her she's wrong. She might not say anything that helps you, but you might learn something about how other people see you that's useful for future friendships. As far as making new friends, having a party usually isn't a good solution. It would be better to just try to be a good friend one-on-one with somebody. Instead of waiting to be picked for class projects, go up to someone and ask her to join you. Or try talking to someone new at lunch. Invite a girl you like to work on homework together after school, or invite someone to the movies. (It always helps to have a planned activity so that there isn't a lot of awkward silence.) When you're hanging out with someone new, try to be pleasant and friendly, not clingy or desperate. And who knows? When your old friends see you laughing with the new ones, they just might want to join the fun!

Dear Ali,

Every time I call one of my friends to do stuff, she makes up excuses about why she can't come, but I know that she's really hanging out with her other friends. When I'm with her, she says she doesn't like the other girls, but I think she probably says the same thing about me to them! I can't ask the other girls in her group, because we don't like each other! What should I do?

—Confused

Dear Confused,

This isn't easy, but friendships always take a bit of hard work to grow strong. You need to ask this girl what's going on. She may feel she can't be up front with you about her friendship with the other girls because you'll want her to choose between you and them. Or she may just be trying to spare your feelings. On the other hand, your talk might confirm your feeling that she's only acting like a friend to your face while bad-mouthing you behind your back. If that's the case, you'll probably want to concentrate on your other friends. Either way, it's always worth it to try talking things through!

ali

Bad Influence?

Dear Ali,

One of my friends has a really bad cussing problem. I hear her cussing so much that I start to cuss, too. Everyone says I've changed since I started hanging around her, and I feel like I have, also. She makes fun of people, and uses cuss words to describe other students, as well as the teacher. I don't like to do any of that. Also, her family is in the process of choosing middle schools and she might go to mine. I just have so many mixed feelings!

—Sick of Swearing

Dear Sick of Swearing,

I read your letter twice to see if you'd said anything good about this friend, and guess what? You didn't. I'm sure this girl has some good qualities, but unfortunately, sometimes you have to decide if the friendship is worth the price. Using cuss words is a bad habit that can get you up to your neck in hot water. You have no control over whether or not this girl ends up in your school, but you can control whether or not you continue to spend time with her. If the friendship is really important to you, you may want to tell her the cussing and being mean really bother you, and give her a chance to change. But if she can't (or won't), it may be time to find some new friends.

ali

Dear Ali,

My best friend is great. She's funny, talks to me when I need someone to talk to, and encourages me a lot about everything. But she also seems to copy me a lot and outdo me a lot. I dance competitively and she tries to do moves that I do, and she does them wrong in a tiny way but everybody always cheers for her—when I taught her how to do them! I know I sound like a snobby brat, and I know that you're going to say to take her copying me as a compliment, but it's hard to do that. She also thinks I'm perfect, so when I do something good, she says something like, "Don't be such a show-off." And I know she thinks I'm pretty, smart, and talented, because she wrote me a letter about it. She needs to find the good things about herself and not copy me. It shouldn't take her too long, because I found them in the first five minutes after I met her.

—Copycatee

Dear Copycatee,

You've solved your own problem and you don't even know it! The last thing you said in your letter is a beautiful tribute to your friend and to how much she means to you. You need to tell her how you feel. It might not be easy, but it's the only way to clear the air. Tell her what an amazing friend she is. Then tell her that it bothers you that she sometimes tries to copy the things you do. And let her know that it hurts your feelings when she puts you down. And, most important, tell her that you wish she'd see the amazing girl she is—and that she doesn't need to copy anyone!

My best friend read my diary!

Dear Ali,

I need help! I invited my BFF for a sleepover and when I was sleeping, she found my diary and read it. It had things in it about boys I like. The next morning, she told me what she had done and promised that she could keep a secret because she was my BFF, so I trusted her. Then on Monday, she told everyone at school and now kids keep teasing me. I told her that if she didn't stop, we couldn't be friends anymore, but she didn't care. I lost all my friends so I started hanging out with the boys. And when I talk to boys, she tells everyone that I like them—and then they won't be my friends, either. I don't know what to do. I didn't know that a BFF I thought I could trust would go behind my back, just like that. Please help me. I'm so confused.

-Betrayed

Dear Betrayed,

A real friend would never do what this girl did. You were right to ask her to stop, and you were right to tell her you couldn't be her friend any longer if she didn't. It won't be easy, but the best thing you can do now is to ignore her and her comments. When she starts spreading rumors or sharing your secrets, just say something like, "I'm flattered that everyone's so interested in my life, but most of what she says isn't true." Then just let it go. If someone says he or she won't be your friend because of what this girl is saying, try saying something like, "I think it's so sad that you would give up being my friend because of her gossip." Dealing head-on with comments is your best bet. With a little time, your ex-BFF will fade out of the spotlight and you'll have some great new friends!

ali

Dear Ali,

I have two best friends and usually we all get along great, but last week they got in a big fight. Every day they both tell me why they are right and beg me to take their side. I keep telling them I don't want to, but they don't stop! I'm really tired of hearing about this stupid fight, and I just want them to be friends again. What should I do?

—Caught in the Middle

✷ ✷ ✷

Dear Caught in the Middle,

It's so unfair of your friends to put you in this position—good for you for sticking to what you know is right! Your best bet is to take each of them aside and tell her that, as much as you value her friendship, you can't take sides because you value the other girl's friendship, too. You could add that you really just wish the three of you could get back to being friends again and ask if there's anything you can do (*besides* taking sides!) to help them make up. Hopefully, they'll find a way to work it out, but if they can't, you can still continue to be friends with each of them separately.

ali

Dear Ali,

I used to live in Missouri, but I recently moved to California. I really hate it here, and I'm not making a very good impression in my class. Two girls in particular are being mean to me. This grade has been together since kindergarten, and they don't want me to make friends. How can I break into a small group and learn to like California more?

—Miserable in Malibu

Dear Miserable in Malibu,

It's always hard to be new in a school when all the other kids have known each other for a long time! You probably won't be accepted by everyone all at once, but making just one friend can make a world of difference. Is there someone in the group that you especially like or who has been a little friendlier than the others? Ask her over after school, maybe to do homework together—that way you'll have something to do and the two of you can talk while you work. You'll probably find it a lot easier to make friends when you're only dealing with one person, not a group. And remember to stay upbeat! If your new classmates get the impression you liked everything better "back home," they might feel like you really don't like them (even if it's not true!).

ali

Need to Breathe!

Dear Ali,

I have a really good friend that I have known since third grade. Lately she has been crowding me and keeping me from being with my other friends at school. My other friends have also noticed. I really want to talk to her, but I don't know how. I don't want our friendship to end because of this.

—Crowded

Dear Crowded,

Even if you're afraid of the worst—in this case, that your friendship will end—the only way for your friend to know you're having a problem with her is for you to talk about it. Having a conversation like that isn't always easy, but here are some guidelines:

- Find a time and place that is private, where you won't be overheard or interrupted.
- Make sure you aren't angry—you want to have a nice, polite discussion.
- Talk about yourself and how you feel. Be careful not to accuse her by saying, "You did this and you did that." Instead, use "I" statements. For example, you might say, "I feel bad that I can't hang out with my other friends sometimes without hurting your feelings."
- If you're having trouble getting started, try imagining that it's all over. Picture yourself someplace fun, totally relaxed, and knowing that you made the effort and had a good conversation.

Dear Ali,

I told my friend some lies because I was trying not to hurt her feelings. Then she figured out that I was lying to her and now she won't talk to me. What can I do to make her talk to me again?

—Liar

☆ ☆ ☆

Dear Liar,

You can't "make" someone talk to you or forgive you. You can only try your hardest to do what you know is right and see what happens. Explain to your friend that you only lied because you were trying to protect her feelings. If she won't listen to you, try explaining yourself in a letter. Be sure to apologize, and remind her how important her friendship is to you.

ali

Money Matters

Dear Ali,

My friend is <u>always</u> borrowing my money! I can't stop it! She is always short a dollar or two and says, "I swear I'll pay you back." The problem is that she never does. It's so hard to bring it up, and she can't take a hint. Please help me!

                                                        —Broke

Dear Broke,

Your friend is a freeloader! And right now she doesn't have any reason to change because the situation is working for her. And *why* is it working? Because you keep loaning her money! I know it's tough—you want to be nice and you want to trust her, but every time you let her borrow money, you're just perpetuating the problem. But don't just cut her off! Let her know (very nicely) what she owes you and that you'll be glad to give her a loan again *after* she's paid you back. Don't sound angry, hurt, or annoyed, just matter-of-fact, and make sure the conversation is private—just the two of you! Spell it out clearly up front, and you won't have to agonize over it every time—just be sure to stick to your rules!

My friend is always borrowing money...

Dear Ali,

I have this friend and she is being really mean to me. She always leaves me out of things in school and it is very upsetting. And I have no parents so it is really, really hard for me. I have to cope with people teasing me because I'm an orphan. I wish they would stop. What should I do?

—All Alone

Dear All Alone,

It can be hard to accept, but if a friend isn't being nice and keeps leaving you out, she has probably moved on. I know it must be especially hard for you to lose a friend since you don't have parents. If you can talk to your caregiver or to another adult you trust, please share your concerns with them and see if they can help you find ways to fit in. When kids make mean comments, you might try confusing them by saying something like, "That's such a sweet thing to say, thank you." Then ignore any further comments. Find kids who *don't* tease, and start to make some new friends. Be open and sincere without being pushy, and you'll find new friends who will include you and be nice. It might take some time, but soon you'll start to feel like you've got some friends who believe in you.

Dear Ali,

I once had two best friends, until one moved away. I thought it would be okay and that I could still talk to Stephanie on the phone and still have Kim over. But once Stephanie moved away, Kim started hanging out with this other girl and started to kind of ignore me. I've invited her over but she just isn't the same. She didn't gradually ignore me, either—she just dropped me like a hot potato. I don't understand why because I haven't done anything to upset her. I want to be her best friend again, but how?

-Left Behind

Dear Left Behind,

It can be tough when friends move, and it sounds like Kim has tried to adjust to Stephanie's absence in her own way. It could be that when she's with you, she misses Stephanie since you three used to hang out together. The only way to find out what's going on for sure is to talk it over with Kim. See if she'll come over and then let her know that you miss spending time with her, and that you'd like to talk about your friendship. Then just ask her, honestly and sincerely, why she's been ignoring you. Hopefully, she'll give you some answers and be open to working on your friendship. If not, at least you'll know what's really going on and you can start finding some new friendships. And, of course, you can still talk and write to Stephanie!

Fab Girls Guide to Getting Your Questions Answered

Chapter Two

Family

When it comes to your family, your biggest fears are:

- Your parents getting a divorce.
- Losing a family member.
- Your parents won't understand you.

Too Busy

Dear Ali,

I have so many activities all the time! I never get to just do nothing or hang out with my friends. My mom always wants me to try everything. I like some of the sports I do but don't really want to do piano, ballet, and swimming, too, but she won't let me quit anything. She just says I'm so lucky to have so many opportunities and I should do my best at everything. Help me, please!

—Overloaded

Dear Overloaded,

It sounds like maybe your mom didn't have all these opportunities when she was a girl, and she wants to be sure that you do. That's wonderful, but you should also make sure she understands how overloaded you feel. Start by telling her how much you love her and that you appreciate all the effort she's put into giving you these opportunities. Next, explain to her that you feel overwhelmed, and when you have so many activities, you can't possibly do your best at all of them. Ask her if you can continue with just two activities for the next few months, and take a break from the others. Suggest that she choose one of the activities and you choose the other, and promise to work especially hard at them. Then make sure you hold up your end of the bargain!

Dear Ali,

I need some advice. My younger sister uses web sites that are too old for her. She's been keeping it a secret, and I've seen her on them more than once. Is there any way that I can get her to stop without her hating me?

—Web-Surfing Sister

Dear Web-Surfing Sister,

Have you tried talking to her? Nicely let her know that you have noticed that she is on some inappropriate sites and you're worried. If you share a computer, you might tell her that you're afraid that you might get in trouble if your parents check the web sites visited on that computer. You might also ask your parents to put parental controls on the computer. You don't even have to mention your sister. Just tell them that when you do a search online sometimes, web sites come up that aren't appropriate for you, and you don't want to have to worry about that. (Of course, this will only work if you and your sister share a computer.) If you still don't get anywhere, you'll have to tell your parents. Your sister may find out and be mad for a while, but she'll get over it. And isn't it worth enduring her anger to keep her safe?

My mom won't let me buy it!

Dear Ali,

Every time my mom and I go shopping for clothes, I see something that I really like that she won't let me have. It could be the saying on the shirt or the pattern on some Capris. I even offer to pay for it myself, but if she doesn't like it, I can't get it. I'm the one wearing the clothes! How come if my mom doesn't like it, I can't get it, even if I pay for it?

—Fashion Foiled

Dear Fashion Foiled,

Wow—what a frustrating situation! If your mom is rejecting your choices because she thinks they're not appropriate for someone your age, you may just have to live by her rules for now. But if you simply have different tastes, you may be able to talk her into a compromise—*if* you handle the situation maturely. *Don't* have this conversation when you are already out shopping! Instead, pick a time when she's not rushed or stressed. Tell her that you've been thinking a lot about this and want to understand her point of view, and that you hope she'll listen to yours. Then listen carefully to what her objections are and try to calmly address them, one by one. Hopefully she'll see that you're growing up and deserve the chance to make some of your own choices.

ali

Problems at Home

Dear Ali,

My parents fight a lot and my dad drinks a lot. My dad will say some little thing and then my mom goes ballistic about it. I'm scared they will get a divorce. I really love both my mom and dad. I don't want anything to jeopardize their relationship. I think I make things worse for them. It must be my fault. Help me, please!

—My Fault

Dear My Fault,

Listen to this really carefully: It's not your fault. As much as you want your parents to stay together, you have no control over their relationship. The best thing you can do is to talk to your parents separately and tell them how upset you get when they fight. If you let them know that you are worried that they might divorce, they may be able to help you understand the situation better. They might say that divorce is not a possibility, or they might confirm your fears that their relationship is in trouble. Either way, they're responsible for what happens between them, and if they do divorce, they'll do the best they can to take care of you. All you can do is love your parents and try to respect their decisions, whatever they are.

ali

Dear Ali,

My parents make jokes about me and tease me, and they think it's funny. They don't know that their jokes really hurt my feelings. I tried telling them how I feel, but they just tell me they're kidding around. Most of the jokes make me feel worthless and some of them just hurt inside. I feel I can't go to my parents for advice anymore. Please help me!

—No Joke

Dear No Joke,

No doubt your parents really *are* just teasing. They don't mean any harm by what they're saying, so it's hard for them to understand how you feel. Since things are unlikely to change unless they *do* understand, you'll have to try one more time (at least) to get your point across. Think carefully about what you want to say. Be sure to tell them that you know they are not trying to hurt you, and that since they love you, you're sure they'll want to know how upset you are. Let them know it's gotten so bad that you feel you can't talk to them anymore, and that makes you really sad. If they *still* don't get it, talk to another adult you trust—a teacher, aunt, cousin, grandparent, or school counselor—who may be able to help your parents understand. Don't give up...you are *not* worthless, and you don't deserve all this hurt.

Unclean Scene

Dear Ali,

My house is such a disgusting mess all the time. My family is really messy. I'm totally embarrassed to have my friends over. I'm afraid they will tell everyone at my school. They already think something is wrong at my house because I haven't had anyone over yet. What can I do?

—Not a Neat Freak

★ ★ ★

Dear Not a Neat Freak,

Wow, that's a tough situation to be in. Try having a serious talk with your family to let them know how important this is to you. Make sure you handle the situation with some tact, though! *Don't* accuse them of being slobs. Instead, tell them you're uncomfortable having people over when the house is messy, and suggest a family clean-up day. If they know this means a lot to you *and* you volunteer to do some of the work, you should get the results you want. If not, you'll simply have to take matters into your own hands and clean, clean, clean! Good luck!

ali

Dear Ali,

My mom and I fight all the time. Sometimes we fight over stupid things, like whether I did my chores or not. Other times, it's about nothing at all. I have gone to several people but none of them have helped. My mom thinks we fight because my parents recently divorced, but that's not it. I don't know what it is or what to do. Please help me!

—Mad at Mom

Dear Mad at Mom,

It's very common for girls to fight more with their moms as they get closer to their teen years. As you become more independent, she worries about keeping you safe, and...well, it's almost inevitable that you'll clash from time to time. It's also possible that your mom is right when she says you're fighting because of your parents' divorce. Even though it doesn't *feel* like that's the problem, you could be angry at her, at your dad, or just at the universe for putting you through all that upset. It might help to tell your mom you really want to get along better. Promise to try to listen to her point of view and tell her you hope she'll try to listen to yours. Hopefully she'll be impressed by your maturity and will meet you halfway. And hang in there—it will get better with time.

ali

Oh, Brother!

Dear Ali,

My problem is my twin brother. My mom thinks we should appreciate each other, but I really don't like him. When I wear nice clothes and make cool things, he says I look ugly or "That's ugly." He steals my stuff, including my library card. He thinks I am a show-off but I don't think I am. Why can't we be friends? Help!

—Unhappy Twin

Dear Unhappy Twin,

Brothers and sisters often fight while they are growing up, only to become friends as adults. Perhaps you and your brother are having a particularly difficult time because, as twins, everyone expects you to be super close. There are some things you can do to try to get along better, but *do* keep one thing in mind: You can't change the way your brother behaves. You can only change how *you* act. If you're up for a challenge, try a little experiment: Treat him nicely for a week. Refuse to fight with him or insult him. Ignore his teasing. You may be surprised to find that if *you* change, he will, too. It's unlikely that you'll stop fighting for good, but there's a good chance you can improve things considerably.

ali

My brother and I don't get along!

Not a Baby!

Dear Ali,

I can't get along with my parents. I'm almost 13 and they won't even let me walk to a park by myself. (The park is less than a block away!) They are too overprotective. My friends say things like, "You'll be thankful later!" But I feel like they're strangling me! I have been wishing they were different since I was seven. How can I make them trust me?

—Overprotected

Dear Overprotected,

Have you asked your parents *why* they're so protective? If it's not because of something you've done and you've never given them reason to distrust your judgment, your best bet is to calmly ask them for a little slack. Be sure to let them know that you understand that they are only trying to keep you safe. Suggest some *small* changes to start, then make sure you stick to any conditions they set forth. For example, maybe they'll agree to let you walk to the park with a friend, or if you call them from a pay phone or cell phone when you get there. If they still won't give an inch, try asking another adult you trust—an aunt, grandparent, or teacher—to help convince them that you're old enough to have a bit more freedom.

ali

Dear Ali,

I've got a big problem. I live with my mom and step-dad. My real dad lives in Mexico, but my stepdad hates it when my real dad calls me. Sometimes I cry and get mad at my stepdad. I don't get why he doesn't let me talk to my real dad. Ali, please help me.

—Missing Dad

Dear Missing Dad,

It's hard being separated from a parent, and not being allowed to speak with your dad must make it even worse. Your best bet is to talk to your mom first. Remind her that you love her and your stepdad, but that you also love your real dad. Tell her that you don't understand why you're not allowed to speak with him. It's possible your stepdad is acting out of concern for you. He may think your dad is not a responsible father, and if so, he may be trying to protect you by keeping you from having too much contact with him. On the other hand, he may just be jealous of your real dad and afraid of losing your love. Until you understand what your stepdad is thinking, it will be hard to solve the problem. If talking to your mom doesn't help, try talking to a school counselor or another adult you trust.

ali

A Pet Plea

Dear Ali,

I have always wanted a dog. I asked for one on my birthday and Christmas, but it's almost spring and still no dog! My parents think they'll be the ones taking care of it, so they won't let me have one. I know I can take care of a dog myself. What should I do?

−Dog Lover

Dear Dog Lover,

As your parents well know, taking care of a dog is a lot of work. They need to be given food and water and walked every day. They make messes that you have to clean up, they're likely to bring more dirt into the house, and most of them shed. You can't let their care slide (even for a day) because you're tired, bored, or sick. Are you really ready for this much responsibility? If so, you need to prove that to your parents. Start by being completely faithful about doing the chores you have now—without being nagged or reminded. Read up on dog ownership, then put together schedules for feeding and walking a dog, so your parents can see how you'd fit caring for your pooch into your day. If possible, arrange to dogsit or walk a neighbor's dog for a few days. If you can show your parents that you're serious about caring for the animal yourself, you'll have a much better chance of becoming a dog owner. Good luck.

Dear Ali,

I'm the youngest in my family and nobody ever listens to me. My opinion doesn't count—they all treat me like I don't know anything at all, but it's not true! How can I get them to listen to me?

-Ignored

Dear Ignored,

You're not alone, believe me! Somehow it's easy for everyone in the family to get in the habit of ignoring the youngest child. There are a couple of ways to be sure you get noticed and listened to, though. First, try speaking to one person at a time—it's harder to command attention if you're trying to silence a whole group! And make sure that you have something positive to say, at least until your family gets more used to listening to your opinions. (If they think you just want to complain, they're likely to tune you out.) Keep speaking up—you're important to your family and have great things to contribute.

ali

My mom listens in on my phone calls!

Dear Ali,

My mom always listens to my phone conversations on speakerphone downstairs while I am upstairs with the phone. I can't stand it! I have asked her to please stop and she just says, "Well, what are you talking about that you don't want me to hear?" Please help. It's embarrassing because my friend and boyfriend ask why she does it. I am almost 13!

-No Privacy

Dear No Privacy,

It sounds like your mom is having a little trouble getting used to the fact that you're growing up! It's possible that she listens in because she feels that's the *only* way she'll find out what's going on in your life. So even though this is probably the *last* thing you want to do now, it may help if you make an extra effort to fill her in on what's happening with you and your friends. (You might even offer to tell her what the conversation was about after you hang up.) Other than that, you need to try talking to her again. Remind her that wanting some privacy with your friends doesn't mean you're talking about anything bad or wrong, and that your friends feel uncomfortable knowing she's listening in. And remember: Present your case calmly. You have good reason to be annoyed, but getting angry will only increase the chances that your mom will think you want to keep your conversations private because you have something to hide.

Dear Ali,

My little sister is getting really mean. If I do one little thing to upset her, she hits me or calls me names. When I tell my parents, they don't believe me because they don't see it or hear it, and because she's littler than I am. What should I do?

—Can't Take It

Dear Can't Take It,

I'm sure most parents—including yours—try to be fair, but it's also often true that the youngest child gets the benefit of the doubt when there's trouble between sibs. If your parents don't believe your sister is acting badly, you may have no choice but to try to change her behavior on your own. The next time she's behaving badly, head for your room and close the door for a while. When you are both feeling calm again, make it clear to your sister that you don't like being with her when she hits you and calls you names. Even more important, try to "catch her in the act" of being good. Praise her for the nice things she does, and tell her how much you like it when she acts that way. Use your head, keep your cool, and use *compliments* as your defense, and you may be able to change her behavior for the better.

ali

Dear Ali,

Every time I lift my arms up, my friends make fun of me because I have hair under my arms. I also have hair on my legs. I already asked my mom if I could shave but she said I was too young. None of my other friends have hair under their arms yet and they are all allowed to shave their legs. I need help, Ali!

—Feeling Hairy

Dear Feeling Hairy,

It's hard when you're developing faster than your friends. It's worth trying to talk to your mom again to see if she'll reconsider letting you shave. Make sure that you approach her at a time when she can really listen to you, and be positive—no whining or begging! Let her know how important this is to you. Tell her that not being allowed to shave makes you feel different from other girls your age and makes you very self-conscious. If she still thinks you're too young to shave, ask her to help you shop for clothes that will allow you to feel more comfortable, like shirts with sleeves, and capris instead of shorts. Maybe your willingness to find another solution will even help your mom see how much the situation disturbs you, but if not, at least your friends won't have as much opportunity to tease you.

ali

Chapter Three

Boys

Your top 3
boy-related
problems are:

- Not knowing if your crush likes you.
- Pressure to have a boyfriend.
- A boy likes you but you don't like him back.

Dear Ali,

I just got a boyfriend and my BFF now hates me and says I don't spend enough time with her! And worst of all, when he comes on the playground, my BFF says, "Here's your cue to ditch me and play with him!" What do I do?

—Stuck in the Middle

Dear Stuck in the Middle,

Sounds like a classic case of "boyfriend-itis"! If your BFF's observations are accurate, you're doing what lots of girls do: Ditching your friends for a crush. Most likely, she doesn't hate you—she's just sad, lonely, and jealous of your relationship with this boy. Try putting yourself in her place: Imagine that she's the one with the boyfriend, and all of a sudden she's with *him* when you wish she were with *you*. See what her problem is? The trick to keeping your friendship strong is to talk it through and make compromises. Let her know that she's still your BFF and that her friendship is important to you. Find ways that the three of you can hang out together, and be sure to spend some time with just her.

ali

Dear Ali,

I have a huge crush on this boy at my school. I've done everything in my power to impress him. I dress nicely and I changed my hairstyle. I even became a basketball fan because he loves basketball. But it's like he doesn't know I exist. He's in some of my classes and I want to talk to him but I always get too nervous. How can I get him to notice me?

—Invisible

Dear Invisible,

Your best bet for getting someone to notice you is just to start up a relaxed, friendly conversation. Easier said than done, huh? So how do you get over those serious butterflies that leave you so tongue-tied? First, try being *yourself*. Instead of dressing up for him or doing your hair just for him, wear something *you* feel good wearing, and do your hair the way *you* like it. It will be easier to relax around him if you feel like yourself. As for the basketball—if he has truly inspired you to become interested in the sport, go for it. But if you're faking an interest just to get his attention, it's bound to fail in the long run. (Besides, wouldn't it be better to have him like the *real* you?) So stop worrying so much about impressing him, and concentrate on just being yourself. As for conversation, start small. Smile and say hi in class. Ask him what he thought of a homework assignment or a quiz. You'll start to feel more comfortable around him, and talking to him will be much easier.

Dear Ali,

I have the biggest crush on this boy, but he's one of my friends. He used to be my closest friend back in fourth grade, then I moved to a new school. Now in seventh grade, we're best buds again. I want to tell him how I feel but I don't know how he feels about me, and I don't want to ruin our friendship. How can I let him know how I feel without endangering our friendship?

—So Confused

Dear So Confused,

This is a tricky situation. Friendship can sometimes blossom into something more, but it's hard to get from friendship to romance without taking some risks. If you confess these feelings to your crush and he doesn't feel the same way, you may end up feeling so awkward around each other that it will be hard to stay friends. On the other hand, if he's also crushing on you and you start going out, how long is it likely to last? When the relationship ends, it will be very hard to go back to being "just" friends. If your feelings are so strong that you feel it's worth it to risk the friendship, go for it. But if you're not sure, it may be better to wait awhile. After all, if you're still crushing on him a few months from now, you can always reconsider. But once you've taken the step of letting him know how you feel, you can't take it back.

ali

I have the biggest crush on this boy...

Still Hoping

Dear Ali,

I like this guy in my class, but he doesn't like me back. We were friends a few years ago and I thought he liked me but I guess I was wrong. My friends say things like, "Why do you like him? You know he doesn't like you!" I've liked him for the past four years but he <u>still</u> doesn't like me. Should I give up on love?

−Desperate

Dear Desperate,

You should *never* give up on love! But sometimes you *do* have to let go of a crush if it's not returned. Sometimes friends can see things that we're not quite ready to see, and it may be that your friends are tired of you crushing on a guy who just isn't going to respond. (They just want what's best for you!) It can be hard to let go and move on, but it sounds like that's what you need to do. Focus on other things in your life, and the people who do give you attention. Hang out with friends, and vow *not* to talk about boys. Read a lot. Do some extra credit projects. Before you know it, someone new might catch your eye—and this time maybe the feelings will be mutual!

ali

Dear Ali,

I have two friends who became boyfriend and girl-friend. At first it was great, but then he started to gang up on me with some other girls. He's always calling me names and making fun of me. I have learned to ignore them, but when he saw that it wasn't making me leave my friend (his girlfriend) he started to tell her lies about me. She and I have talked about it, but she says she has to see him <u>do</u> something in order to take sides. I need some help!

—BFF's BF Problem

Dear BFF's BF Problem,

Whoa! Several things are happening here. First, I'd bet that the boyfriend is jealous of your friendship with his girlfriend. It sounds like he wants her to just focus on *him* and not on her girlfriends. And if your girlfriend doesn't believe you when you tell her what's going on, maybe she's not as close a friend as you thought. It might be a good idea to spend time with other friends until she gets her priorities straightened out. Sometimes we do lose sight of friendships when we're interested in a boy—but in the end, it's those friendships that matter the most! Hopefully, she'll get it sorted out and realize that she needs to show you a little more loyalty.

ali

Tongue-Tied

Dear Ali,

I have a crush on a boy. I want to talk to him but I am too shy to even look at him for very long. I want to be able to talk to him and look at him for longer than two seconds. Can you help me?

—Shy Girl

Dear Shy Girl,

Shyness can be hard to overcome, but with a little practice you can do it. First of all, tell yourself that it's okay to talk to him and to look at him, just like you look at and talk to your other friends. Come up with some things you'd like to say to him and write them down. These can be as simple as saying hi or asking about a homework assignment—they don't have to be brilliant conversation starters. For the next few days, take a few minutes several times a day to imagine that you are looking at him and talking to him. Picture doing it until you can do it comfortably in your mind. Imagine that it goes perfectly. Lastly, picture yourself after you've talked to him, feeling happy and pleased with how well it went. After several days of rehearsing it in your mind, try it out in person. Start with the simplest thing—saying hi. You just might be amazed at how easy it is!

ali

Dear Ali,

I have a weird problem. I'm 12, and I have a crush on my best friend's brother. The problem is that he's only 11 and in the grade below us. I can't even tell my best friend, because I'm afraid she'll laugh at me. She thinks he's just a dumb little kid. I don't even want to like him but I'm at her house a lot so I see him all the time. I just can't stop thinking about him. Should I tell her how I feel?

—Secret Crush

Dear Secret Crush,

If you've been good friends for a long time and your BFF has always been loyal to you, you might not be giving her enough credit. Has she respected your feelings in the past? If so, take a chance and tell her—just make sure she knows you're feeling sensitive about this. On the other hand, if she has a history of being insensitive, you're probably better off not sharing this information with her. Either way, it might help if you try hanging out at *your* house for a while so you don't see quite so much of her brother. And remember, there's one good thing about crushes—they usually don't last very long. Chances are you'll be crushing on someone else soon, and your friend's brother will seem like yesterday's news.

Ali

My friends want me to have a boyfriend...

Dear Ali,

My friends have boyfriends and we're only 10! They keep trying to get me to hook up with this guy I really like, but I'm not ready to have a boyfriend. Every time we have a fight, they say I'm jealous because they have boyfriends, but I'm not jealous. I would really like to have a boyfriend at some point, but I'm not ready. Should I go ahead and have a boyfriend, or should I wait?

—Being Pushed

Dear Being Pushed,

Some girls like a special boy when they're eight and some girls don't find someone they care about until college. There are no rules about when to have a boyfriend, so you need to do what feels right for you. Don't make a big deal out of it when your friends suggest that you hook up with your crush. Just say something like, "Thanks for trying to help, but I'm just not interested." The trick is not to get worked up. If your friends just can't understand, you might want to start developing some new friendships with girls who aren't so focused on boyfriends.

ali

Same Guy!

Dear Ali,

I used to have a crush on the same guy as my best friend, but I never told her because she might get mad. Then a couple of weeks ago she started going out with him. I try not to like him so much but I can't help it. I'm really jealous, and I don't want to be around her when she's talking about him (like, all the time). I think she knows something's wrong, but I can't tell her what it is. How can I stop liking him? Help!

—Crushed

Dear Crushed,

Unfortunately, you can't make yourself feel (or not feel) something. You can, however, try to distract yourself from your feelings. Try not to hang out with your BFF and her boyfriend, or be around him any more than you have to. Keep busy with other activities so you don't have time to think about him, and put some effort into making friends with other guys. In addition to all that though, you should also talk to your friend, even if it is scary. Look at it this way: She already knows something is wrong, so she's probably imagining it's something even worse. Be sure to tell her how important she is to you and to reassure her that you have no intention of acting on your crush by, for example, flirting with him. You might also ask her not to talk about him too much around you, or ask you to hang out with the two of them. Then give her some time to get used to the idea. She'll come around...and with time, your feelings for him will fade.

Dear Ali,

I have a crush on a boy in my class. The problem is that he is my best guy friend. The problem is also that I <u>used</u> to like him and then I stopped, and I told him that I don't like him anymore—but now I like him <u>again</u>! Should I tell him?

—On Again, Off Again

Dear On Again, Off Again,

Hmmm...are you confused? Chances are this boy is! Sounds like you've got a good friendship going, so before you complicate matters by telling him you've changed your mind again, stop and think. Why did you stop liking him? Why did you start again? Is this really about your feelings for him, or are you just enjoying the drama? (Be honest!) If you sincerely like him and are willing to risk your friendship to go out with him, tell him how you feel. Otherwise, it might be wiser to keep your lips zipped.

Dear Ali,

I'm the only girl on my soccer team, but I'm not that great. The boys are always telling me how bad I am, and it really upsets me. I'm even thinking about quitting, but I really want to play. What should I do?

—Soccer Sad

Dear Soccer Sad,

You're a true sport for hanging in there in the face of those critical boys! The most important thing is that you *keep playing!* You can't control how they treat you, but you can work on not letting their words upset you. More to the point, you *can* work on your soccer skills and, yes, improve! If you practice hard and keep playing, you *will* get better. And when the boys realize you're serious, they'll tease you less and give you the respect you deserve. Just don't let them chase you away from doing something you love. Instead, look at this as a challenge and keep on kicking. And good luck!

ali

Dear Ali,

There is this boy who has been my friend. Then one day he told me that he likes me! I never had feelings for him before, but now I think I like him. Are these feelings real or what? I don't want to think I like him if it's only because he said he likes me. What should I do?

—Unsure

Dear Unsure,

Boys and crushes...confusing stuff, huh? It's possible you *do* like this boy, but it took hearing that he has a crush on you to make you think of him in that way. But it's also possible that you just like the *idea* of having a boyfriend, and you've convinced yourself you like him because you know he likes you, so...*voilà!* Instant boyfriend! Ultimately, you're the only one who can decide what's going on. So sit yourself down and ask yourself these questions:

- If you stay "just friends" and he gets a girlfriend, will you be jealous?
- Do you want a boyfriend just because it seems like everyone else does?
- Do you think having a boyfriend would make you more popular—and is that important to you?

Take your time, and be honest with yourself! You'll figure out what you truly want.

ali

He likes me... I don't like him.

Dear Ali,

This guy in my class likes me, but I don't like him. He's telling all his friends that I like him. He wrote a note to me asking me to be his girlfriend. I just want to work on schoolwork and not worry about having a boyfriend. Anyway, I'm too young to be thinking about that. How do I make him stop? I've tried everything.

—No Boyfriend for Me

Dear No Boyfriend for Me,

You can't make this boy stop liking you, but hopefully your actions can discourage him enough that he'll keep his feelings to himself. Even if you've talked to him already, try doing so one more time. Don't make a big deal of it—just find a minute when you have his attention and say something like, "I'm sorry, but I really don't want a boyfriend right now, and I only want to be friends." If it's too hard to tell him face-to-face, write a very brief note. And let that be the end of it as far as you are concerned. Make sure your girlfriends know clearly where you stand—if they do, it won't matter what he says to people. He might keep on sending you notes and gossiping, but if you don't respond, odds are good that he'll stop.

ali

I Want Out!

Dear Ali,

All my friends ever talk about is their boyfriends. I got tired of always being left out, so when this boy in my class asked me out, I said yes. It was okay at first but I'm getting really sick of it now. He always wants to hang out at school, and he IM-s me at night and he even brings me presents sometimes. I don't want to hurt his feelings, but I don't want a boyfriend anymore. What do I do?

—Tired of BF

Dear Tired,

You need to tell him. His feelings might be a little hurt at first, but it's better to tell him the truth than to let him go on thinking you like him as much as he likes you. (And it sounds like he really does like you!) Just tell him nicely that you enjoy being friends with him but you've realized that you're just not ready to have a boyfriend yet. And the next time a boy asks you out, think about how you really feel before saying yes. If you like the *idea* of having a boyfriend more than you like the boy, tell him you're not interested.

ali

Dear Ali,

I have a huge crush on this boy at my school. He's really, really cute, and he always cracks jokes and makes me laugh. I really want to know if he likes me back but I'm afraid to ask him. How can I tell?

—Totally Crushed

Dear Totally Crushed,

If he cracks jokes when you're around, that's a good sign—he's probably trying to get your attention and likes making you laugh. Sometimes boys do drop little hints like that. He might also try to find excuses to be near you or to talk to you, like passing your desk on the way to the pencil sharpener four times a day, or IM-ing you every night for the math assignment. He might also tease you more than he teases other girls, although hopefully not in a mean way. (Boys aren't all that mature in middle school.) On the other hand, some boys are too shy to drop hints, so it's entirely possible that he likes you even if he *doesn't* do these things. (Confusing, huh?) You *could* go the time-honored route of asking one of your friends to ask one of his friends, but it may not be the best idea. (If he says no, everyone involved will know you've been rejected...ugh.) Sometimes it's better to wonder...and hope.

ali

Chapter Four

School

When it comes to school, you worry most about:

- Fitting in.
- Balancing your many activities.
- Getting bullied.

Want to Improve

Dear Ali,

I used to be a straight-A student. Now I feel my grades are dropping, but only in math. I'm great in every other subject. But I still want to do better. My friends look up to me and I usually help them when they need help on something, but now I can't. I'm scared to even show them my grades. I guess I just don't understand math anymore. How can I do better?

—Math Frazzled

Dear Math Frazzled,

It sounds like you're a great student! If you've been used to getting good grades without much effort, it can be frustrating the first time you really have to work for a grade, but that doesn't mean it's time to give up. So, how do you tackle the problem? First, try talking to your teacher. Explain that you want to do your best, and ask her how you can get some extra help. If you're worried about your grade, ask if there's some extra-credit you can do. In the meantime, be proud of the effort you put forth, and keep on working with your friends. They won't think less of you for having to work harder, and you may even be able to help each other. So figure out what's wrong, work to change it, and don't give up on yourself so easily!

ali

Dear Ali,

I have a problem. I am going to a new middle school in September, and I am scared that I will not be able to get to the right classes on time and that I will be late for every class. The other problem is that I am going from a tiny grade school to a really big middle school and high school. What if I get lost or can't find my locker?

—Scared Student

Dear Scared Student,

A lot of kids feel this way when they're starting a new, bigger school, so you're not alone. Many schools have an orientation day for the new class coming in to make that first day less scary. They'll probably give you a map and help you find your locker and your classrooms. If your school doesn't have an orientation day or you just want to be extra sure you'll know your way around, ask your parents to call the school and arrange to visit during summer break. Also, don't stress out thinking you'll be late and get in trouble. As long as you're careful not to stop and chat between classes, you should have enough time to get where you're going.

ali

Anything for Friendship?

Dear Ali,

There is a girl in my class that I really want to be friends with. She is more popular than I am at school, but we go to the same church and sometimes we hang out there. Sometimes she is nice to me at church but most of the time she ignores me at school. Last week we were taking a Spanish test and she started looking at my answers. I told her not to, but she made this sad face so I let her. Afterwards she said I could sit with her and her friends at lunch. I want to be her friend but I don't want to be a cheater. What should I do?

—Not a Cheater

Dear Not a Cheater,

You're right not to want to be a cheater, so don't let this girl turn you into one! If she's only nice to you when she wants something from you, she's using you. You may enjoy being a little more popular for a little while after you help her out, but is that really worth losing your self-respect? Stay true to what you know is right, and stick to real friends who like you for who you are, not what you can do for them. You deserve no less.

ali

I want to be friends, but I don't want to cheat!

War of the Words

Dear Ali,

A lot of people in my school call me really bad names. I try to ignore them, but I just can't because it hurts my feelings. I need some advice!

—Hurting

Dear Hurting,

Words can hurt, and it's hard to ignore them. There are two approaches to this kind of problem. One is to ignore them, which is hard to do, as you've found out! It might help to think of the comments as rain that just washes over you and drains away—it can't hurt you or stay with you. Another approach is to surprise the name-callers with a new and unexpected response. Remember, they're trying to feel important by making you uncomfortable. If it doesn't work, they may stop. So smile back and say, "I like being me just fine, thanks," or "Have a nice day!" In the meantime, remember what a terrific girl you are, and that they are the ones with the real problem, not you! And if all else fails, find a moment to talk to your teacher when other kids aren't around—she should be able to help.

ali

Dear Ali,

I have a huge problem focusing on schoolwork. When I'm at school it's a little easier because there aren't as many distractions, but at home it's a disaster. My brothers call me a procrastinator and I'm starting to agree with them. I can't focus. A few years ago the doctor said I probably have ADD, but the next year my teacher said I am "too smart" to have it. Anyway, how can I concentrate? Can you help me?

—Procrastinator

Dear Procrastinator,

First, decide right now that you're not going to label yourself a procrastinator! Instead, try making a few changes at home. You should have an area that's just for homework—a table or desk that's quiet, well-lit, and away from any distractions like people, music, or television. Then, do your assignments one at a time. When it's time to do math, take out *only* the things you need for math. When that's done, put everything away and take out only what you need for the next subject. As you complete each assignment, give yourself a little reward: Listen to one song on your iPod, read five pages of a fun book, or play with your cat for five minutes. If you really try but still don't see an improvement, ask your parents for help. It may be time to consult your doctor again, or find a tutor to help you study.

ali

I need help in math...

Dear Ali,

My grades in math are really low because I didn't get math during sixth grade. But in a few months I'm going to seventh grade. How am I going to understand that kind of math without knowing the other? I also asked for tutoring programs after school, but I still don't get it. All the other kids, even my friends, get it but I don't, and my teacher is a little harsh sometimes.

—Math Dummy

Dear Math Dummy,

You may be having trouble with math, but you're no dummy. It's very smart of you to ask for help at the tutoring program and to recognize that you need *more* help to succeed next year. It's important that you continue to push the adults in your life to get you that help. Start with your parents: Tell them that you're frustrated but that you don't want to give up. Ask them if you can work with a private tutor over the summer. If that's not possible, talk to your seventh grade math teacher on the first day of school and let her know that you want extra help to catch up. (She'll probably be impressed with your maturity and determination.) You might even ask your friends for help, too. Everyone's brain works differently, and you probably just need to find someone who can explain the concepts in a way that makes sense to you. If you keep trying, you'll get there.

Dear Ali,

I love to be involved at school. I'm on the yearbook staff, on student council, and in a book club, and I have a couple of other activities, too, plus one thing at church. I also want to join a school sports team and start guitar lessons, but if I were in sports I would have to give up a lot of other activities. And my mom says I can't take guitar lessons because I've got too much on my plate, but I think I could take it once a week. What should I do?

—Overwhelmed

Dear Overwhelmed,

It's amazing that you're so involved! Try making a list of everything, including the activities you'd *like* to be doing. Put them in order of how important they are to you. Then add a note next to each about how much time and/or money it takes, and when you'll need rides. Having it all written down will help you see how much of a time commitment you and your mom are making, as well as how balanced your activities are. Go over your list with your mom and try to come to an agreement on which activities are best for you. (Be prepared to fight for your top choices!) This will show your mom that you've thought this through and understand the commitments you're both making.

ali

Dear Ali,

The kids at my school like me because of my things, not because of who I am. Even though I show them what a good person I am, they don't care! What should I do?

-Liked for the Wrong Reasons

Dear Liked for the Wrong Reasons,

Wow—you're asking an important and tough question! It sounds like you may need to place less importance on your possessions for a while in order to strike a better balance with your friends. Try inviting them to do something other than come to your house and play with your stuff. Arrange to meet at the park, or go to the mall or the movies. Spending more time away from all your things will help you to feel more comfortable and give your friends a chance to get to know the real you better.

She calls me names and yells at me!

Dear Ali,

There's a girl at school who's always mean to me. She calls me names, bugs me, and yells at me! I want her to leave me alone. I'm scared to compete against her, because I'm worried I'll lose and she'll make fun of me. I've already told the teacher and tried ignoring her, and I even tried talking it out with her, but nothing seems to stop her. It's getting so I don't want to go to school anymore. What should I do?

—Tried Everything

Dear Tried Everything,

This girl is definitely the one with the problem—but unfortunately, she's taking it out on you! You've already tried lots of great options to work this out. If talking to your teacher hasn't helped, it's time to get your parents involved. Ask if the three of you can have a conference with your teacher. The harassment should not be allowed to continue. If your school has a "peer mediation" group, you might ask to try this option also. In that case, you and the girl would talk with the help of someone your own age who does not take sides and who helps each of you to see the other's point of view.

ali

Dear Ali,

I'm really smart in school. My teacher makes up review games for tests, and when I go against someone, they always say, "Oh, I'm gonna lose. I better just not play." It hurts my feelings. One day, I even let someone win because they said that. I like being smart because of good grades, but I don't want to be picked on. (I do have friends, and my best friend always sticks up for me) What should I do? Get over it and hang out with my real friends, or act stupid for the rest of my life?

—Miss Einstein

Dear Miss Einstein,

When you put it that way, it seems like an easy choice: Hang out with your real friends and show your smarts! It's understandable that your feelings get hurt, but it would be much better to develop a thicker skin than to hide your brains. Here's something else you might try: The next time someone says there's no point in playing against you, toss her a compliment. For example, you might say something like, "Yeah, math does come easy to me, but I can't run as fast as you." You could also show her you're not that concerned about who wins by saying, "Besides, I just want to get ready for the test. It doesn't really matter who wins." Being generous toward the other person may help her feel less insecure. And if all else fails, think about this: If you're going to be teased about something, isn't it better that it's for a positive quality, like being smart?

Dear Ali,

I have a lot going on, and I keep forgetting about my homework. I'm really busy taking care of my family's new puppy, doing chores, and being involved with my friends. Plus my parents keep telling me to clean my room. I try to be neat but then my room gets messy again. It's the same drill every day. At the end of the day I'm so tired that I forget about my homework. Help me, please.

—Too Busy

Dear Too Busy,

Sounds like it's time to reorder your priorities! If you leave your homework until the very end of the day, you're bound to be too tired to do it well—or even to do it at all. It *is* important to get your chores done, and that puppy is counting on you for good care, but your schoolwork really should come before being involved with your friends. Try getting your homework and chores done as soon as you get home from school. Write up a schedule of your assignments and chores, and as you finish each item on it, check it off. After everything is done, you can relax and hang out with your friends.

Chapter Five

Body Issues, Growing Up, and Self-Esteem

Growing up is tough!
You're worried that:

- You're the first—or the last—to develop.
- You need to lose weight.
- You can't keep up with all your responsibilities.

Dear Ali,

My friend Anaya is very chubby, and everyone is always making fun of her just because she is overweight. We work out and she lost 35 pounds, but everyone still makes fun of me for hanging out with her. I'm starting to think there's something wrong with me. Am I doing the right thing? I need advice.

—Teased Friend

Dear Teased Friend,

There's nothing wrong with you—in fact, you're a great friend! It's always the right thing to stand by your friends when others are teasing. And not only are you standing by Anaya, you're helping her to get healthier by working out together! If someone makes fun of you for hanging out with her, either ignore them completely, or say something like, "She's a good friend." Either way, keep your response brief and matter-of-fact. If they see they can't get you upset, the teasers will stop.

Dear Ali,

I'm going through puberty and my mood changes a lot. For example, I was playing with my friend and I was all happy and everything. Then, all of a sudden, I got really mean and he said, "If you don't stop being mean, I'll just go home!" I didn't know what to do! What can I do about it?

—Moody Girl

Dear Moody Girl,

Moodiness *is* a part of puberty. Your body is producing all kinds of new hormones, and unfortunately they can put you on an emotional roller coaster. You can't do much about that, but you *can* be extra careful about how you act around friends and family. If you feel a bad mood coming on, it's okay to retreat to your room for a while. It will also help to have an outlet for your feelings, such as writing poems or songs, drawing, or playing or listening to music. If a bad mood gets the best of you and you say something you regret (and it happens to everyone), apologize immediately and explain that you didn't mean it. Hang in there—before long your hormone levels will even out, and you'll be able to get off that roller coaster and feel normal again.

ali

Changing Too Fast

Dear Ali,

We just watched the sex education tape in school. I'm the only girl in my class with a chest. So when it came to the part about breasts and bras, all the girls started looking and even pointing at me. Now I feel really awkward around everyone, even my best friends. I'm not sure how to react or what to say. Please help me!

—Awkward Outcast

Dear Awkward Outcast,

You don't have to say anything, actually. Just ignore the girls who aren't your friends; they're probably just curious—or envious!—and didn't mean to hurt your feelings or make you feel self-conscious. You don't have to say anything to your best friends, either, if you prefer not to. But if you trust them not to tease you, you might feel better if you clear the air. Tell them you feel a little awkward being the first to develop. They will all be going through the same thing soon enough, and it will help all of you if you can talk about it. Isn't that what are friends for?

I'm the only girl in my class with a chest.

Overweight and Okay?

Dear Ali,

I'm fat. It seems weird for me to be saying this. I don't know if people talk about how fat I am behind my back, but I don't care. At least I used to not care. I used to think, "This is who I am," and "People have to accept me for the way I am, and if they don't, that's up to them." Should I still follow the rule that "If my friends try to change me then they aren't really my friends?" Can you help me? I weigh 220 pounds and I'm 11.

—Fat

Dear Fat,

Do you feel like your friends are trying to change you because they are sincerely concerned about your well-being and happiness? The fact that they mention your weight does not necessarily mean that they are not good friends. What's important is why they've brought it up. They may sincerely want you to be healthier, to be active in sports, and to be able to wear cute clothes. They may even be concerned that your feelings could be hurt by other kids teasing you about your weight. If that's the case, they have your best interests at heart and are still your friends. But if they mention your weight in a mean way and seem to want to hurt your feelings or put you down, they're not acting like true friends.

ali

Dear Ali,

I've been playing soccer for four years, and I love it. But this year I joined a new team, and I'm nothing like the other girls! I'm not skinny, and when I miss a shot, they all yell at me! My mom keeps telling me, "Be yourself." Well, I've been myself my <u>entire</u> <u>life</u> and it's still not working. I feel like a loser. Can you help?

—Soccer Loser

Dear Soccer Loser,

Hey—*you're not a loser!* You sound like a girl with a great sense of who you are, and your mom is right: You should go on being your amazing self. So what else can you do? You and your mom might try having a talk with the coach. Explain that you're uncomfortable with all the negative comments when you miss a shot. Ask the coach to talk to the team, not about you specifically, but about how teammates should treat each other. Keep projecting a positive self-image and doing what you love (playing soccer), and the other girls will accept you for who you are, even if you're not just like them.

ali

Dear Ali,

All of my brothers and sisters say that I'm fat, but my mom does not. But sometimes I think that she's lying to me. I think maybe I am fat, but I don't know who to believe.

—Am I Fat?

Dear Am I Fat?,

Sometimes brothers and sisters say thoughtless things. You need to sit down with your mom and discuss the situation. Tell her that you honestly want to know if you are too heavy to be healthy. If talking to your mom doesn't reassure you, ask her if she can make an appointment with your doctor, who can tell you if your weight is in the normal, healthy range for your age and height. If you need to lose weight, your doctor can help you. But if it turns out that your brothers and sisters are just being mean, tune them out. What matters is what you know to be true.

Dear Ali,

I don't feel good about myself. When I look in a mirror, I feel like breaking it. I think the reason I don't have friends is because I'm ugly. I even have a paper in my pocket that says, "I hate myself!" I want to feel good about myself, but I feel miserable. I even cry about this! Please, Ali, help me!

—Hating Myself

Dear Hating Myself,

The first thing you need to do is to take that piece of paper out of your pocket, tear it up, and throw it away. Then write a new note that says, "I love myself," and put that in your pocket instead. From now on, take that note out of your pocket five times a day and read it. You also need to talk to an adult about how you feel. We all have moments when we feel down on ourselves, but you shouldn't go through life hating yourself. If you can't talk to your mom or dad, is there a teacher, guidance counselor, or coach at school that you can talk to—someone who listens to you and who you trust? Or maybe an aunt or a grandparent? Ask to talk to her privately, and then explain your feelings. If the first person you talk to doesn't help you, try someone else. Be brave enough to keep asking for help, because there is help out there. You deserve to feel good about yourself—and if you keep trying, you will.

Dear Ali,

I never want to grow up. I just want to stay the same forever. My friends think I'm really weird since I read comics and watch cartoons like a little kid, and even my mom says I <u>have</u> to grow up. Every time I'm with my friends, I have to hide my real hobbies and what I like. It doesn't interfere with my education, so I can't see why I should start growing up, just because my friends and family want me to.

—Forever Young

Dear Forever Young,

Everyone "grows up" at different times and in different ways. There are adults who never really grow up in the way some people might think they should, and kids who grow up much too fast in some ways. Whether we like it or not, things do change—no one can stop time from passing. But that doesn't mean you have to give up your interests. In fact, it's really cool that you've stuck with what you like, in spite of the pressure to change. Maybe you could try doing some babysitting—that way you'd be doing a grown up thing, but you would also be playing with younger kids who have the same interests as you.

ali

A "Big" Problem

Dear Ali,

My friend Kaitlyn and I are taller than most kids in our grade. We're also the only two girls in our grade who are more developed physically. I often look at my other friends and think how incredibly petite and skinny they are. And sometimes popular girls and guys tease me, saying things like, "You're gross! You have big jugs!" or snapping my bra strap constantly to embarrass me. One even grabbed a pad from my backpack and laughed. And they only do it to me, not Kaitlyn! I'm getting tired of it! Please help!

—Annoyed at My Body

Dear Annoyed at My Body,

It's always tough to be the first girl in a group to hit puberty. Keep in mind that kids tease because they want attention, they're jealous, or they think putting someone else down makes them cool. In other words, their teasing has more to do with what's going on with them than anything to do with you. Still, it might help to look at how you're reacting to them. They may go after you instead of Kaitlyn because you get more upset, and they think it's fun to watch you react. Instead of getting angry or embarrassed, act like it's no big deal. Even better, try a little humor. When someone comments on your size, say something like, "Really? Wow—I hadn't noticed." It won't be easy, but if you can muster up your courage and stand up to the teasing, it should slow down and eventually stop. And your final revenge? Everyone else *will* catch up!

I'm tired of being picked on...

Feeling Different

Dear Ali,

I used to wear leg braces because of the way I walked. If I didn't wear them, I would have had to get an operation. Now I have to wear them again. My friends and other people in my grade always ask me questions about them. It really hurts my feelings and I get embarrassed. I want to be treated just like everyone else because I have been called names my whole life. Help!

—Braced

Dear Braced,

It's terrible that you've been called names your whole life—that stinks! But like it or not, people are going to be curious about your leg braces, and their questions aren't necessarily an attempt to be mean. If it seems like they're just curious, answer them briefly and directly. You might say something like, "I have a problem with my legs and these braces are helping to correct it." You don't have to tell them any more than that if you don't want to. If they keep asking questions, tell them you appreciate their interest but you'd much rather talk about something else. As for the teasers, I know it's not easy, but ignore them. The more you show that you accept your leg braces and aren't bothered by them, the more other people will accept them, too.

Dear Ali,

I'm in the advanced math class at my school, and there's this girl in my class who is so much smarter than I am. She's always first to finish math problems, she always aces tests, and she always does extra credit on her homework. Aside from all of that, she is a junior professional dancer. She's been in "The Nutcracker" about a million times. It makes me feel so dumb and untalented. Is she wicked smart or am I just really dumb?

—Feeling Dumb

Dear Feeling Dumb,

It sounds like this girl *is* smart and talented...and it also sounds like you're jealous. That's a natural emotion, and you're not the first girl who has ever felt it—we all have. But here's the thing about life: You can *always* find someone smarter, prettier, or more talented than you are, but why look at the world like that? Her many gifts do not detract from your talents and abilities—and you *do* have them. The trick is to think about who you are, not who she is. If you want to get better grades in math or learn how to dance, figure out what you need to do to reach those goals. But do it because you want to be the best you can be, not because you're jealous of her.

ali

Chapter Six

Tough Stuff

Your toughest "Top 3"

- Your parents' divorce.
- Having someone you love die.
- Keeping a really big secret.

Problem Dad

Dear Ali,

My dad is an alcoholic, and he travels a lot for his work. My mom says that they can never live together because my dad can only stay sober for about seven days. He barely comes home, and most of his money goes to alcohol. I miss him a lot and I don't know what to do. Everyone is always talking about how much fun they have when they spend time with their dads but I can't. And my dad always calls when he's drunk and he makes me cry and then my mom and dad get in a fight. What should I do?

—Drunk Dad

Dear Drunk Dad,

Alcoholism is a very difficult disease to deal with, and no one can really help your dad until he decides he's ready. Until he *is* ready to get help, your mom is doing the right thing by not letting him live with you. You also should not have to talk to him when he's drunk. It will be difficult, but the best thing you can do for yourself right now is to tell him, "Dad, I love you, but I don't want to talk to you when you've been drinking. It upsets me too much." Hopefully your dad will be ready to get help soon, for your sake as well as his own. In the meantime, you might ask your mom to look into Alateen, a program for kids with alcoholic parents. Alateen can help you understand his problem better, and teach you the best ways to deal with it.

ali

Dear Ali,

I feel so lonely. My dad passed away last year, and now my mom is always partying, going on dates, or on the computer. She never pays any attention to me. My brothers don't like me, either—they wish I were somewhere else. I don't have any friends. I used to think some of the girls in a grade above me were my friends, but lately they seem to be avoiding me. I don't have anybody to talk to, share my feelings with, or hang out with. I need some advice.

—Totally Lost

Dear Totally Lost,

I'm so sorry to hear about your dad—it's really hard to lose someone so important to you. Try writing a letter to your mom explaining that you really miss her and wish you could spend more time together. Focus on the positive things you'd like to do together, rather than complaining about her dates or other activities. Then ask your teacher if you can speak to a school counselor—talking about your feelings will help you feel better. (The counselor won't share what you say with anyone else, unless you want her to.) As for friends, invite over a girl in your own grade. If you don't click with the first girl you ask, invite someone else. It may take some time, but if you remember to stay open and positive (don't get clingy), you will surely find a friend your own age to trust and confide in. And remember, although you will always miss him, as time passes your sadness about your dad will become easier to bear.

I don't want to choose...

Can't Choose!

Dear Ali,

My parents are divorced and now I have a stepmom who really loves me, but my mom doesn't want me to accept her. But I love her and when I'm 12 I have to choose my mom, or my dad and stepmom. What should I do? I only have 2 years to decide. Please help me, Ali.

—Two Moms

Dear Two Moms,

I'd bet anything that your mom is scared of losing you. She thinks that if she keeps you from accepting your stepmom now, you won't leave her later on. You need to talk to your mom. Tell her, very calmly, that you love her very much and that you will always be her daughter, but that you love and need your dad, too. Remind her that although you care about your stepmom, she could never take your mom's place. Try to help your mom see that your stepmom isn't a threat to her, but something good for you. (How could you ever have too many people to love you?) And don't worry too much about having to make the decision now. You'll do a lot of growing in the next two years, and you'll be much more ready to decide when the time comes.

ali

Out-of-Control Friend

Dear Ali,

I have a friend who is my age (11), and she is going out with her next-door neighbor, who is 17. She isn't even supposed to be going out! She threatens everybody if they try to tell. She said the 17-year-old has already kissed her! He takes her shopping and everything. I have no clue what to do! Please Ali, help me!

—Unsure

Dear Unsure,

It's understandable that you don't want to tell on your friend, but it sounds like you have good reason to be worried about her. So—in spite of the girl's threats—this is one of those times when it's okay to betray a confidence. Tell your parents or an adult you trust what's going on. Yes, it may cost you the girl's friendship, at least for a while. But think about it: If a friend is truly headed for trouble, isn't letting an adult know the right thing to do?

ali

Dear Ali,

Lately I've been worrying a lot. I'm afraid terrorists are going to bomb my house or blow up my neighborhood. Or maybe there will be a hurricane and my house will get destroyed. Then I can't get to sleep. My mom says to just not think about it, but I don't know how to stop.

—Can't Sleep

Dear Can't Sleep,

You're certainly not alone—a lot of people are worried these days. It's particularly hard to deal with fears about things we can't control, and nighttime always seems to make everything scarier. The best thing you can do is to talk about your fears during the daytime. Just getting your feelings out in the open can make them seem much less overwhelming. It may also help to remind yourself that no matter how terrible the evening news is, we live in a very safe country. No one can give you a guarantee that everything in your life will be okay, but the chance of anything bad happening to you because of terrorists or hurricanes is very, very small. And finally, avoid watching the news or scary shows at night. Instead, try watching a show—or better yet, reading a book—that makes you laugh. You'll get to sleep more easily.

ali

My best friend has cancer, and I want to help.

Dear Ali,

I just found out that my best friend has cancer. I want to talk to her about it but I don't know what to say. I feel so nervous whenever I am around her. I am afraid I will say the wrong thing and make her feel worse. I am so sad and I want to help her so badly, but I don't know what to do.

—Want to Help

Dear Want to Help,

Your friend is lucky to have a friend who cares so much about her. The best thing you can do is to tell her how you feel. Explain that you care about her and that you want to help, but you're afraid of saying or doing the wrong thing. Ask her what she'd like you to do, and then honor her wishes. If she wants to talk about what she's going through, be there to listen. If she doesn't want to dwell on it, find fun things to do to distract her from her troubles. Whatever you do, stick by your friend—the *last* thing she needs is to lose her best friend on top of everything she's going through. Talking about how you feel will be awkward at first, but you'll *both* feel better if you do.

ali

Dad Doesn't Understand

Dear Ali,

I suffer from anxiety and when I have to leave the house, I start to get sick. We got a therapist to help my anxiety go away. My parents are divorced and my dad dislikes my therapist. My dad makes me mad a lot, but the most recent thing was when he said that I was worthless if I didn't try to get over my anxiety. He is a nice guy but he really hurts me inside. How do I tell my dad how I feel? I don't want to hurt his feelings.

—Not Worthless

Dear Not Worthless,

Your dad may be a nice guy sometimes, but it's not very nice of him to tell you you're worthless, no matter what he thinks of your therapist or your anxiety problem. He should know how his comments make you feel, even if it does hurt his feelings. Have you talked to your therapist about telling him? Since she knows all about your relationship with your dad, she's probably the best person to help you figure out exactly what to say. You might also want to talk to your mom and your therapist about taking a break from visits with your dad for a while. You need to be surrounded by loving, supportive people while you're working through your anxiety, and it doesn't sound like he's acting that way.

ali

Dear Ali,

My mom smokes and tries to hide it from me. She'll go downstairs or in the garage to smoke. I have heard all kinds of bad things smoking can do to you. It makes me sad to hear that. I want to tell her all the bad things it will do to her but I always get scared she will get mad at me. What should I do?

—Cigarette Hater

Dear Cigarette Hater,

No doubt your mom already knows how unhealthy smoking is—that's probably one of the reasons she hides it. She doesn't want you to smoke, so she doesn't want to set a bad example by smoking in front of you. She probably does not want you to inhale "second-hand smoke" by being around her when she's smoking, because that's unhealthy, too. Instead of telling her how bad cigarettes are, tell her that you love her no matter what, but that you want her to be healthy and it would mean a lot to you if she quit. Then ask if there is anything you can do to help. And remember: You can't convince her to quit. All you can do is tell her how you feel. The rest is up to her.

ali

Can't Trust Him

Dear Ali,

My stepdad has been away for a while with his work. He even missed my birthday. At first, my mom told me that his work took him all the way to the other side of the country, but she just told me that he's really been in jail for about a month. I'm really mad at him. He sent some illegal things through an e-mail and he <u>knew</u> that was illegal. He knows I need him in my life, but he did it and hurt my mom and me anyway. I don't know if I can ever trust him again. Can you please help me?

—Bad Stepdad

Dear Bad Stepdad,

I'm sure your stepdad wasn't *trying* to hurt you. Nevertheless, you have every right to be angry with him, and it's understandable that you no longer trust him. *Do* tell him how you feel. Make it clear that you love him and need him in your life, and you're angry with him for doing something that makes it so hard for him to be there for you. Hopefully he'll work hard to be more honest and prove he is worthy of your trust again. No matter what, it will take time for your relationship to mend—don't expect things to change overnight. In the meantime, make sure you have someone to talk to about your feelings. You'll feel better if you do.

ali

My stepdad is in jail.

Dad Doesn't Care?

Dear Ali,

My mom died a year ago and my dad does not care about her anymore. He's dating a teacher that I kind of like, but sometimes they have parties and show off, and I hate that! What should I do?

—Sad for My Mom

☆ ☆ ☆

Dear Sad for My Mom,

I'm so sorry that your mom died. That's something you will always be sad about, and I'm sure your dad will, too. And yet, as hard as it is to do, you both need to move on with your lives. I doubt your dad has really stopped caring about your mom. Instead, he may have decided that he needs to make a happy new life for both of you. It will help to talk to your dad about how you feel. He may not realize how upset you are, and he can probably reassure you that your mom is still very much in his heart—as she will always be in yours.

Dear Ali,

I don't know what to do. I think my friend's dad is hurting her. One time she called and she was crying. She said, "He hit me again." But then the next day she said she didn't mean it and that she was just mad. But she sounded really upset and like she meant it, and she even had bruises on her arm. And she had more bruises yesterday. If I tell, she will get mad at me, but I don't want her to get hurt.

—Scared Friend

Dear Scared Friend,

You're a good friend for being so concerned. This is one of those situations where you *must* tell an adult. It's hard to know exactly what's going on with your friend, and it's really not something you can figure out on your own. Talk to your parents and let them know how worried you are. You should also tell a teacher, your school counselor, or the principal. If there are signs that your friend is being abused, they will help her. Your friend may be upset if she finds out that you told someone, but you will know you did the right thing by helping to keep her safe.

© 2007 Discovery Girls, Inc. All rights reserved.

Why Are Friendships So Confusing?

She knows everything about you...she'd never tell your secrets...she's your biggest fan. Who doesn't want a friend like that? True friendship is a gift... but it can be hard to find. Whether you're stuck in a fading friendship, caught in the popularity trap, or dealing with mean girls, we'll break down the solutions to your problems step by step. Best of all, we'll teach you how to free yourself from poisonous friendships forever and be the best friend you can be. Soon, you'll be meeting new people and making friends who truly respect and understand you...because you deserve first-rate friendships.

Getting Unstuck

Remember when you got up the courage to tell your crush you liked him...and found out he didn't like you back? Didn't you wish you knew someone who had all the answers? Well, have no fear! Not only do we know exactly how to handle your crush (what is wrong with him, anyway?), but we also know how to deal with a gazillion other sticky situations. Like when your BFF blabs your deepest secret to the entire school...or when you make a total fool of yourself onstage. We'll also tell you how to handle being cornered by a mean dog...or stranded at the mall...and much, much more! By the last page, you'll be ready to deal with anything!

Getting Over Bad Days

Aubrie's best friend told her they couldn't be friends anymore because Aubrie was "too weird" to be seen with. Torrie was so upset when her parents divorced, she gained 20 pounds and let her grades go into free fall. Mackenzie watched her mom grow sicker and sicker and then die, just when Mackenzie needed her most. **In these amazing true stories,** girls just like you share their private struggles, hoping to help *you* through *your* most difficult times. **You'll find comfort,** encouragement, and inspiration here...and best of all, you'll know that **whatever life throws at you, you are never alone.**

Discovery Girls...the magazine that gives you confidence—inside *and* out.

iParenting Media
Award Winner

Free issue!*

- **Advice** on friendship, school, boys & more

- **Quizzes!** Contests! Fun!

- Hilarious **embarrassing** moments

- Cool **fashion** ideas

- Your favorite **celebs**

- **Starring girls** like *you*!

*To order and for details, visit DiscoveryGirls.com.